Biblical Cartoons
for Church Publications

Biblical Cartoons for Church Publications

Dwight Allen, Jr., cartoonist
George W. Knight, compiler

BAKER BOOK HOUSE
Grand Rapids, Michigan 49516

© 1993 by Dwight Allen, Jr.

Published by Baker Book House Company
P.O. Box 6287, Grand Rapids, Michigan 49516-6287

ISBN 0-8010-0228-1

Printed in the United States of America

A Humorous Approach
to Teaching the Bible

Church newsletter editors have learned that cartoons are a great way to attract the attention of their readers. Many people who won't read a serious paragraph or article will take the time to chuckle over a cartoon.

The cartoons in this compilation are sure to get your readers' attention, but they are also designed to go a step further—to teach important truths about the Bible. Dwight Allen, Jr., a Christian lay leader from Bethesda, Maryland, created these cartoons for that specific purpose.

"Although the cartoons are humorous, they reflect a respect for the book on which they are based," he assures us. "I hope they will encourage more reading of the Bible."

All these cartoons are copyright-free, so there is no need to write for special permission to use them. Print them in your church newsletter/worship bulletin or post them on the bulletin board for the enjoyment and edification of church members.

Dwight dedicates this book to his parents, Lillian Ermis Allen and Dwight Allen, Sr. He says he inherited his artistic ability from his mother and his sense of humor from his father. And he admits that several of these cartoons are based on ideas contributed by his father. We're delighted to present these biblical cartoons to give you a different perspective on the Bible and a renewed appreciation for its timeless message.

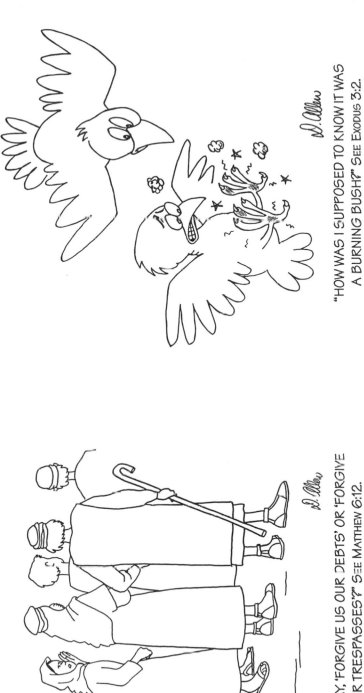

"HOW WAS I SUPPOSED TO KNOW IT WAS A BURNING BUSH?" SEE EXODUS 3:2.

"DID HE SAY, 'FORGIVE US OUR DEBTS' OR 'FORGIVE US OUR TRESPASSES'?" SEE MATTHEW 6:12.

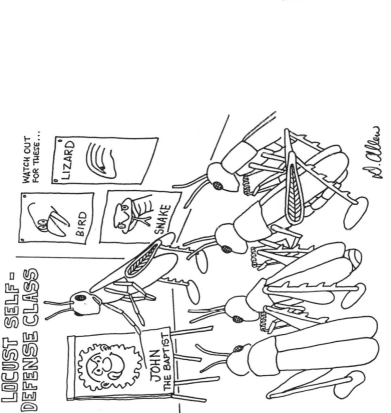

LOCUST SELF-
DEFENSE CLASS

WATCH OUT
FOR THESE...

BIRD

LIZARD

SNAKE

JOHN
THE BAPTIST

"HUMANS GENERALLY AREN'T A THREAT, BUT
THERE IS THIS ONE EXCEPTION . . ." SEE MATTHEW 3:4.

RESTAURANT

"THAT'S JONAH. MAYBE YOU SHOULDN'T MENTION
TODAY'S FISH SPECIAL." SEE JONAH 1:17.

"DID HE SAY, 'FORGIVE US OUR DEBTS' OR 'FORGIVE US OUR TRESPASSES'?" See Matthew 6:12.

"HOW WAS I SUPPOSED TO KNOW IT WAS A BURNING BUSH?" See Exodus 3:2.

"HUMANS GENERALLY AREN'T A THREAT, BUT THERE IS THIS ONE EXCEPTION . . ." See Matthew 3:4.

"THAT'S JONAH. MAYBE YOU SHOULDN'T MENTION TODAY'S FISH SPECIAL." See Jonah 1:17.

"IF THIS KEEPS UP, WE'LL HAVE TO PUT ON EXTRA
HELP JUST TO "PROCESS PAUL'S LETTERS.""

"DON'T ANY OF YOU HAVE A THORN IN YOUR PAW
I COULD REMOVE?" SEE DANIEL 6:16.

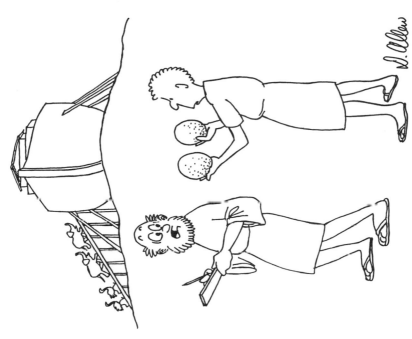

"NOT CANTALOUPE! I SAID TO BRING ME A PAIR OF ANTELOPE!" SEE GENESIS 7:9.

Lamppost Library & Resource Center
Christ United Methodist Church
4488 Poplar Avenue
Memphis, Tennessee 38117

"STOP RUNNING AROUND THE ARK. YOU'RE MAKING EVERYBODY SEASICK." SEE GENESIS 6:19–20.

"DON'T ANY OF YOU HAVE A THORN IN YOUR PAW I COULD REMOVE?" See Daniel 6:16.

"IF THIS KEEPS UP, WE'LL HAVE TO PUT ON EXTRA HELP JUST TO PROCESS PAUL'S LETTERS."

"STOP RUNNING AROUND THE ARK. YOU'RE MAKING EVERYBODY SEASICK." See Genesis 6:19–20.

"NOT CANTALOUPE! I SAID TO BRING ME A PAIR OF ANTELOPE!" See Genesis 7:9.

"BETTER START POURING ON THE OVERTIME. IT'S JUST TWO WEEKS UNTIL METHUSELAH'S BIRTHDAY."
SEE GENESIS 5:27.

"SO MUCH FOR THE IDEA THAT JEREMIAH WOULD BE A FUN GUY TO GIVE THE AFTER-DINNER SPEECH." SEE JEREMIAH 9:13–22.

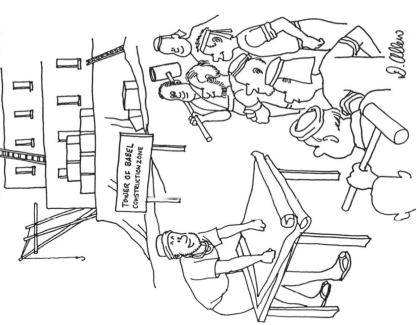

"MEN, I KNOW WE'VE HAD A LOT OF PROBLEMS ON THIS PROJECT, BUT I SEE NOTHING BUT SMOOTH SAILING FROM HERE ON." See Genesis 11:1–9.

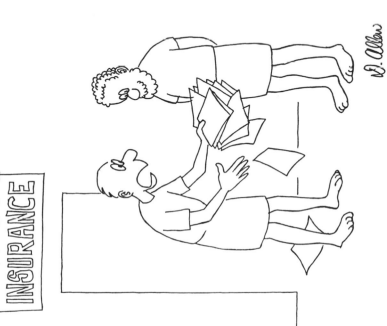

"GET DOWN TO THE TEMPLE AND FIND OUT WHAT HAPPENED. WE'RE GETTING ALL THESE CLAIMS FROM MONEY CHANGERS." See Matthew 21:12.

"SO MUCH FOR THE IDEA THAT JEREMIAH WOULD BE A FUN GUY TO GIVE THE AFTER-DINNER SPEECH." SEE JEREMIAH 9:13–22.

"BETTER START POURING ON THE OVERTIME. IT'S JUST TWO WEEKS UNTIL METHUSELAH'S BIRTHDAY." SEE GENESIS 5:27.

"GET DOWN TO THE TEMPLE AND FIND OUT WHAT HAPPENED. WE'RE GETTING ALL THESE CLAIMS FROM MONEY CHANGERS." SEE MATTHEW 21:12.

"MEN, I KNOW WE'VE HAD A LOT OF PROBLEMS ON THIS PROJECT, BUT I SEE NOTHING BUT SMOOTH SAILING FROM HERE ON." SEE GENESIS 11:1–9.

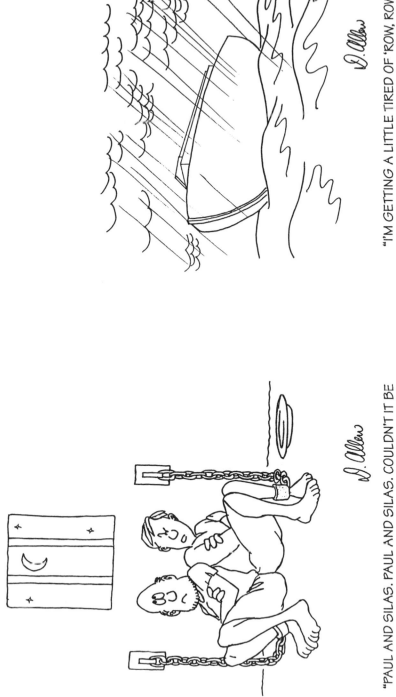

"I'M GETTING A LITTLE TIRED OF 'ROW, ROW, ROW YOUR BOAT.'" SEE GENESIS 7:17.

D. Allen

"PAUL AND SILAS. PAUL AND SILAS. COULDN'T IT BE SILAS AND PAUL JUST ONCE?" SEE ACTS 16:25.

D. Allen

"I HATE TO BRING THIS UP, BUT HOW DO WE KNOW THE WALLS OF JERICHO WON'T FALL *OUTWARD?*" SEE JOSHUA 6:20.

"FOUR HUNDRED AND THIRTY YEARS IN CAPTIVITY—AND WE HAVE TO LEAVE TWO DAYS BEFORE THE SENIOR PROM." SEE EXODUS 12:41.

"PAUL AND SILAS. PAUL AND SILAS. COULDN'T IT BE SILAS AND PAUL JUST ONCE?" See Acts 16:25.

"I'M GETTING A LITTLE TIRED OF 'ROW, ROW, ROW YOUR BOAT.'" See Genesis 7:17.

"FOUR HUNDRED AND THIRTY YEARS IN CAPTIVITY—AND WE HAVE TO LEAVE TWO DAYS BEFORE THE SENIOR PROM." See Exodus 12:41.

"I HATE TO BRING THIS UP, BUT HOW DO WE KNOW THE WALLS OF JERICHO WON'T FALL OUTWARD?" See Joshua 6:20.

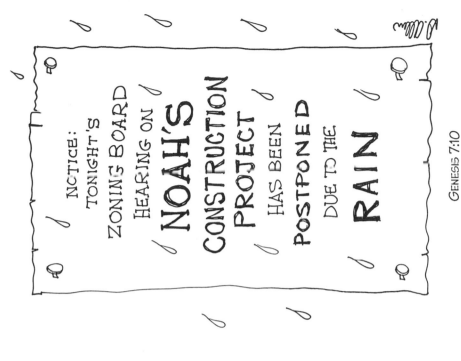

NOTICE:
TONIGHT'S
ZONING BOARD
HEARING ON
NOAH'S
CONSTRUCTION
PROJECT
HAS BEEN
POSTPONED
DUE TO THE
RAIN

GENESIS 7:10

A PRACTICAL JOKE IN BIBLE TIMES.

"YOU'D GET GOOD HISTORY GRADES, TOO, IF METHUSELAH WERE YOUR UNCLE." SEE GENESIS 5:27.

"GO SIT ON THE WINDOWSILL, EUTYCHUS. MAYBE THAT WILL KEEP YOU AWAKE." SEE ACTS 20:9–12.

A PRACTICAL JOKE IN BIBLE TIMES.

NOTICE:
TONIGHT'S
ZONING BOARD
HEARING ON
NOAH'S
CONSTRUCTION
PROJECT
HAS BEEN
POSTPONED
DUE TO THE
RAIN

GENESIS 7:10

"GO SIT ON THE WINDOWSILL, EUTYCHUS. MAYBE
THAT WILL KEEP YOU AWAKE." SEE ACTS 20:9–12.

"YOU'D GET GOOD HISTORY GRADES, TOO, IF
METHUSELAH WERE YOUR UNCLE." SEE GENESIS 5:27.

"SAMSON MUST BE GETTING OLD. I JUST SAW HIM DOWNSTAIRS LEANING AGAINST A PILLAR."

SEE JUDGES 16:29–30.

"NOAH MAY BE A GREAT SHIPBUILDER, BUT HE DOESN'T KNOW A THING ABOUT ANIMALS."

SEE GENESIS 7:13–16.

"MOSES, TO MAKE EAGLE SCOUT, YOU'LL HAVE TO WORK ON TWO THINGS: LEADERSHIP SKILLS AND A SENSE OF DIRECTION." See Numbers 12:3.

"HMM, NO SCHOOLING, NO SKILLS, NO CONNECTIONS. I'D SAY YOUR CAREER OPTIONS ARE FISHING OR BECOMING AN APOSTLE." See Acts 4:13.

"NOAH MAY BE A GREAT SHIPBUILDER, BUT HE DOESN'T KNOW A THING ABOUT ANIMALS." See Genesis 7:13–16.

"SAMSON MUST BE GETTING OLD. I JUST SAW HIM DOWNSTAIRS LEANING AGAINST A PILLAR." See Judges 16:29–30.

"HMM, NO SCHOOLING, NO SKILLS, NO CONNECTIONS. I'D SAY YOUR CAREER OPTIONS ARE FISHING OR BECOMING AN APOSTLE." See Acts 4:13.

"MOSES, TO MAKE EAGLE SCOUT, YOU'LL HAVE TO WORK ON TWO THINGS: LEADERSHIP SKILLS AND A SENSE OF DIRECTION." See Numbers 12:3.

"BALAAM'S BACK—AND HE EITHER WANTS HIS MONEY BACK OR A NON-TALKING MODEL."
SEE NUMBERS 22:28.

"A DISCIPLE'S LIFE ISN'T EASY, BUT AT LEAST WE HAVE MATTHEW TO DO OUR TAX RETURNS."
SEE MATTHEW 9:9.

"HOW DO WE GET BACK? THE WHOLE WAY HERE, WE JUST FOLLOWED THAT STAR." See Matthew 2:1–12.

"FORGET IT, GUYS. GOLIATH HAS ALREADY BEEN THROUGH THE LINE." See 1 Samuel 17:4–7.

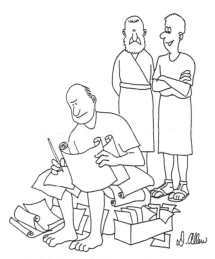

"A DISCIPLE'S LIFE ISN'T EASY, BUT AT LEAST WE
HAVE MATTHEW TO DO OUR TAX RETURNS."
SEE MATTHEW 9:9.

"BALAAM'S BACK—AND HE EITHER WANTS HIS
MONEY BACK OR A NON-TALKING MODEL."
SEE NUMBERS 22:28.

"FORGET IT, GUYS. GOLIATH HAS ALREADY BEEN
THROUGH THE LINE." SEE 1 SAMUEL 17:4–7.

"HOW DO WE GET BACK? THE WHOLE WAY HERE, WE
JUST FOLLOWED THAT STAR." SEE MATTHEW 2:1–12.

BUMPER STICKERS IN BIBLE TIMES

I'D RATHER BE
DANCING

HERODIAS'S DAUGHTER
(MARK 6:22)

I'D RATHER BE
HUNTING

NIMROD (GENESIS 10:9)

I'D RATHER BE
JOGGING

AHIMAAZ (2 SAMUEL 18:19–27)

DANIEL WAS NEVER AGAIN COMFORTABLE
AROUND CATS—OF ANY SIZE. SEE DANIEL 6:16.

DEAR DIARY: 382 DAYS SINCE WE LEFT EGYPT. ALL THE ADULTS HAVE WRITER'S CRAMP FROM SIGNING PETITIONS AGAINST MOSES. SEE NUMBERS 11:1–15.

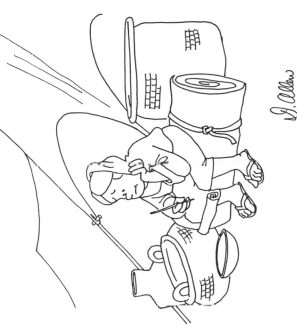

JERICHO CONSTRUCTION COMPANY

"THE BOSS SAID TO PULL THE JERICHO WALL FILE AND BRING HIM THE BUILDER'S WARRANTY."

SEE JOSHUA 6:20.

BUMPER STICKERS IN BIBLE TIMES

I'D RATHER BE
DANCING

HERODIAS'S DAUGHTER
(MARK 6:22)

I'D RATHER BE
HUNTING

NIMROD (GENESIS 10:9)

I'D RATHER BE
JOGGING

AHIMAAZ (2 SAMUEL 18:19–27)

DANIEL WAS NEVER AGAIN COMFORTABLE
AROUND CATS—OF ANY SIZE. SEE DANIEL 6:16.

JERICHO
CONSTRUCTION
COMPANY

"THE BOSS SAID TO PULL THE JERICHO WALL FILE
AND BRING HIM THE BUILDER'S WARRANTY."
SEE JOSHUA 6:20.

DEAR DIARY: 382 DAYS SINCE WE LEFT EGYPT. ALL
THE ADULTS HAVE WRITER'S CRAMP FROM SIGNING
PETITIONS AGAINST MOSES. SEE NUMBERS 11:1–15.

"SHE'S RIGHT, METHUSELAH. SOME OF YOUR IDEAS ARE A LITTLE ANCIENT." SEE GENESIS 5:27.

"AS A MATTER OF FACT, THAT FELLOW JESUS DID COME BY HERE." SEE MARK 1:16–20.

"I LIKE THIS 'GO THE EXTRA MILE' IDEA."
SEE MATTHEW 5:41.

"NONE FOR ME, THANKS. SINCE JONAH, I'VE BEEN TRYING TO BREAK THE HABIT." SEE JONAH 1:17.

"AS A MATTER OF FACT, THAT FELLOW JESUS *DID* COME BY HERE." See Mark 1:16–20.

"SHE'S RIGHT, METHUSELAH. SOME OF YOUR IDEAS ARE A LITTLE ANCIENT." See Genesis 5:27.

"NONE FOR ME, THANKS. SINCE JONAH, I'VE BEEN TRYING TO BREAK THE HABIT." See Jonah 1:17.

"I LIKE THIS 'GO THE EXTRA MILE' IDEA." See Matthew 5:41.

"PAUL IS FINALLY OUT OF ACTION. NOW ALL HE'S
DOING IS WRITING LETTERS."

"I WIN! YOU HAVE TO TELL SAUL THAT DAVID HAS
SLAIN HIS TEN THOUSANDS." SEE 1 SAMUEL 18:7–9.

"JOEL WENT INTO BETHLEHEM TO FIND ANOTHER JOB. HE WAS BORED AT SITTING OUT HERE WITH NOTHING EVER HAPPENING." SEE LUKE 2:8–15.

Mene
Mene
Tekel
Upharsin

"THE CATERER SAYS SHE'LL DO THE CLEANUP, BUT THERE'S A SPECIAL CHARGE FOR THE WALL." SEE DANIEL 5:5, 24–25.

"I WISH YOU HAVE TO TELL SAUL THAT DAVID HAS SLAIN HIS TEN THOUSANDS." See 1 Samuel 18:7–9.

"PAUL IS FINALLY OUT OF ACTION. NOW ALL HE'S DOING IS WRITING LETTERS."

Mene
Mene
Tekel
Upharsin

"THE CATERER SAYS SHE'LL DO THE CLEANUP, BUT THERE'S A SPECIAL CHARGE FOR THE WALL." See Daniel 5:5, 24–25.

"JOEL WENT INTO BETHLEHEM TO FIND ANOTHER JOB. HE WAS BORED AT SITTING OUT HERE WITH NOTHING EVER HAPPENING." See Luke 2:8–15.

"THE NILE'S BLOODY WATER WAS AWFUL! I HOPE WE NEVER HAVE TO GO THROUGH ANYTHING LIKE THAT AGAIN." SEE EXODUS 8:6.

"JUST AS WE GET THE BUSINESS CARDS PRINTED, THE GUY TELLS US TO CHANGE THE NAME FROM SAUL TO PAUL." SEE ACTS 13:9.

PRINTING
AND
ENGRAVING

"THERE JUST WASN'T ROOM FOR THAT COUPLE FROM NAZARETH. A HUNDRED YEARS FROM NOW, WHAT DIFFERENCE WILL IT MAKE?" SEE LUKE 2:7.

"THEY'RE STILL COMING, KING SOLOMON. TODAY IT LOOKS LIKE A DOG, A JUMP ROPE, A CAT, AND A BALL." SEE 1 KINGS 3:16—28.

"JUST AS WE GET THE BUSINESS CARDS PRINTED, THE GUY TELLS US TO CHANGE THE NAME FROM SAUL TO PAUL." SEE ACTS 13:9.

"THE NILE'S BLOODY WATER WAS AWFUL! I HOPE WE NEVER HAVE TO GO THROUGH ANYTHING LIKE THAT AGAIN." SEE EXODUS 8:6.

"THEY'RE STILL COMING, KING SOLOMON. TODAY IT LOOKS LIKE A DOG, A JUMP ROPE, A CAT, AND A BALL." SEE 1 KINGS 3:16–28.

"THERE JUST WASN'T ROOM FOR THAT COUPLE FROM NAZARETH. A HUNDRED YEARS FROM NOW, WHAT DIFFERENCE WILL IT MAKE?" SEE LUKE 2:7.

"SAMSON? BURNING BRANDS? YOU EXPECT ME TO BELIEVE A STORY LIKE THAT?" SEE JUDGES 15:1-5.

"GIDEON, HAVE YOU SEEN MY GOOD FLEECE?" SEE JUDGES 6:36-40.

"JESUS AND HIS FATHER CHARGED ME LESS THAN THEIR ESTIMATE FOR THAT DOOR. NOW THAT'S A MIRACLE." SEE MARK 6:3.

"THERE'S A BIG TRAFFIC JAM UP AHEAD. I OVERHEARD SOMETHING ABOUT THE WATERS BEING PARTED." SEE EXODUS 14:21.

"GIDEON, HAVE YOU SEEN MY GOOD FLEECE?"
See Judges 6:36–40.

"SAMSON? BURNING BRANDS? YOU EXPECT ME TO
BELIEVE A STORY LIKE THAT?" See Judges 15:1–5.

"THERE'S A BIG TRAFFIC JAM UP AHEAD. I
OVERHEARD SOMETHING ABOUT THE WATERS
BEING PARTED." See Exodus 14:21.

"JESUS AND HIS FATHER CHARGED ME LESS THAN
THEIR ESTIMATE FOR THAT DOOR. NOW THAT'S A
MIRACLE." See Mark 6:3.

BETHLEHEM
PUBLIC SCHOOL

"THAT DAVID IS TOO MUCH. I ASKED THE CLASS TO WRITE ABOUT WHAT I DID THIS SUMMER' AND HE TURNED IN SOME WILD TALE ABOUT KILLING A GIANT." SEE 1 SAMUEL 17:20–51.

WATER
DEPARTMENT

"THIS HAS TO BE THE BEST EXCUSE I'VE EVER HEARD. LAZARUS SAYS HE DIDN'T PAY HIS WATER BILL BECAUSE HE WAS DEAD WHEN IT ARRIVED." SEE JOHN 11:1–44.

"ESAU DOESN'T SEEM TO HAVE MUCH TASTE FOR POTTAGE ANYMORE." SEE GENESIS 25:29–34.

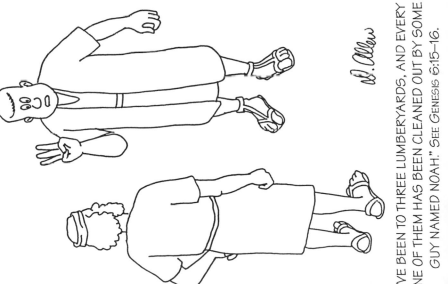

"I'VE BEEN TO THREE LUMBERYARDS, AND EVERY ONE OF THEM HAS BEEN CLEANED OUT BY SOME GUY NAMED NOAH." SEE GENESIS 6:15–16.

"THIS HAS TO BE THE BEST EXCUSE I'VE EVER HEARD. LAZARUS SAYS HE DIDN'T PAY HIS WATER BILL BECAUSE HE WAS *DEAD* WHEN IT ARRIVED." SEE JOHN 11:1–44.

"THAT DAVID IS TOO MUCH. I ASKED THE CLASS TO WRITE ABOUT 'WHAT I DID THIS SUMMER' AND HE TURNED IN SOME WILD TALE ABOUT KILLING A GIANT." SEE 1 SAMUEL 17:20–51.

"I'VE BEEN TO THREE LUMBERYARDS, AND EVERY ONE OF THEM HAS BEEN CLEANED OUT BY SOME GUY NAMED NOAH." SEE GENESIS 6:15–16.

"ESAU DOESN'T SEEM TO HAVE MUCH TASTE FOR POTTAGE ANYMORE." SEE GENESIS 25:29–34.

"GOLIATH HAS ONE BAD DAY, AND THERE GOES OUR UNDEFEATED SEASON." SEE 1 SAMUEL 17:51–52.

"YOU'RE SO SWEET TO CARRY MY SCROLLS HOME FROM SCHOOL FOR ME."

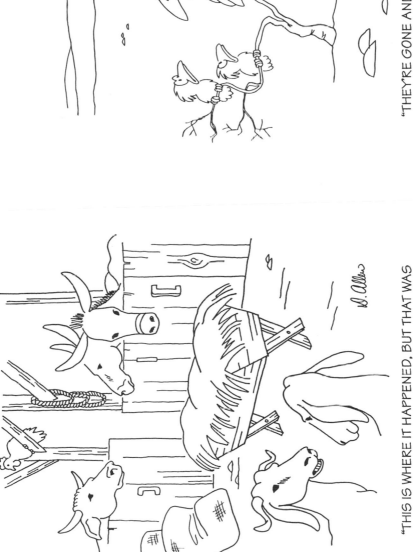

"THEY'RE GONE AND SO IS THE MANNA. NOW I GUESS IT'S BACK TO SEEDS AND SPIDERS." SEE NUMBERS 11:7–9.

"THIS IS WHERE IT HAPPENED, BUT THAT WAS YEARS AGO AND NOBODY HAS HEARD FROM THAT FAMILY SINCE." SEE MATTHEW 2:13–15.

"YOU'RE SO SWEET TO CARRY MY SCROLLS HOME
FROM SCHOOL FOR ME."

"GOLIATH HAS ONE BAD DAY, AND THERE GOES
OUR UNDEFEATED SEASON." See 1 Samuel 17:51–52.

"THIS IS WHERE IT HAPPENED, BUT THAT WAS
YEARS AGO AND NOBODY HAS HEARD FROM THAT
FAMILY SINCE." See Matthew 2:13–15.

"THEY'RE GONE AND SO IS THE MANNA. NOW
I GUESS IT'S BACK TO SEEDS AND SPIDERS."
See Numbers 11:7–9.

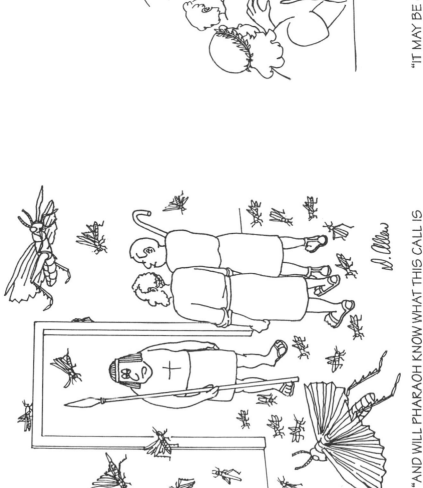

Mene Mene Tekel

"IT MAY BE CURTAINS FOR US, BUT IT'LL MAKE A GREAT FIGURE OF SPEECH." SEE DANIEL 5:5, 25.

"AND WILL PHARAOH KNOW WHAT THIS CALL IS ABOUT?" SEE EXODUS 10:3–16.

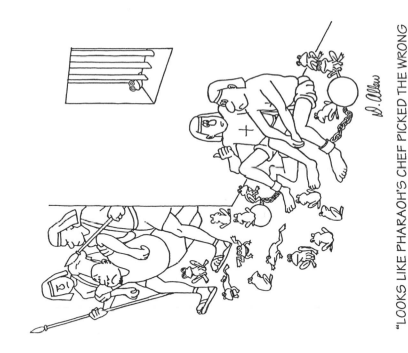

"LOOKS LIKE PHARAOH'S CHEF PICKED THE WRONG NIGHT TO PUT FROGS' LEGS ON THE MENU." SEE EXODUS 8:6.

"FORTY YEARS WE'VE BEEN WANDERING IN THE WILDERNESS, AND THE KIDS ARE STILL ASKING, 'ARE WE THERE YET?'" SEE NUMBERS 14:26–33.

"AND WILL PHARAOH KNOW WHAT THIS CALL IS ABOUT?" See Exodus 10:3–16.

"IT MAY BE CURTAINS FOR US, BUT IT'LL MAKE A GREAT FIGURE OF SPEECH." See Daniel 5:5, 25.

"FORTY YEARS WE'VE BEEN WANDERING IN THE WILDERNESS, AND THE KIDS ARE STILL ASKING, 'ARE WE THERE YET?'" See Numbers 14:26–33.

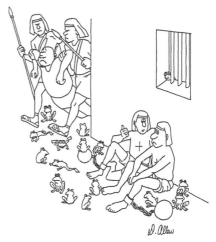

"LOOKS LIKE PHARAOH'S CHEF PICKED THE WRONG NIGHT TO PUT FROGS' LEGS ON THE MENU." See Exodus 8:6.